Struggle & Redemption

Xavier Scott Preston
"Electi A Deo"

BookLeaf
Publishing

Presentation by *BookLeaf Publishing*

Web: www.bookleafpub.com

E-mail: info@bookleafpub.com

ISBN: 9789357212700

First edition 2023

This book is dedicated to my entire family and the memories of Donte Moses Preston, Charmika Carter Preston, and Daisy Boyd. These three were literally angels in human form that showed me how to live life with joy in spite of their disabilities.

I would be remiss if I did not use this opportunity to honor the memory of God's newest angel. My Great Grandmother Edna Wright transitioned from this life to be with the Lord on February 3, 2023. I hope to heed the words of Paul to Timothy and emulate the example of faith she modeled throughout her life by stirring up the gifts God has given me (2 Timothy 1:3-7).

This book is also dedicated to anyone who has ever spoken life or death to me. Whether they wanted to see me succeed or fail, every person I've come across in this life has been a source of motivation in some way and for that, I say thank you!

ACKNOWLEDGEMENT

In an effort to make sure no one is forgotten or feels more important than others, I will acknowledge groups rather than name specific individuals.

First and foremost I want to thank God for entrusting me with the gifts of poetry to bring glory to His name.

Second, I would like to recognize all of my family. Thank you for all of your love, encouragement, correction, and prayers. I am so blessed to have a village and a strong support system that has helped me become who I am today. I hope I'm making you all proud!

A major shoutout goes to Bridging The Gap Urban Ministries (BTG). This is the ministry God used to help bring forth and stir up the gift of poetry/spoken word that was hidden within me. Y'all definitely made me feel loved and helped me to grow so much during my college days. I am forever grateful for you all and the time spent together in ministry.

A huge thank you goes out to my Mt. Sinai Baptist Church family. You all have poured so much into me and have been instrumental in my spiritual growth since I was a child. I just hope I can bless others the way you all have and continue to bless me on a daily basis. Also shoutout to the MSBC Youth Ministry. It is a privilege to serve with a great group of adult leaders and help young people understand and become who they are in God. I also have to say a huge thank you to Mrs. Gloria Carrol for taking time out of her schedule to help edit and provide feedback on several pieces in this book.

Last but certainly not least, I want to shout out WAN Poetry in Houston, Texas. Through your Facebook group, you all have given me the opportunity to perfect my craft by connecting with other great poets and participating in bi-yearly writing challenges that have helped produce several pieces featured in "Struggle and Redemption." Please know you are making an impact that extends far beyond H-Town.

PREFACE

This book came into existence by just writing down ideas inspired by what I've read in the Bible, my life experiences, and things I've noticed taking place in the world. My hope with this book is to encourage readers to remain strong in, renew, or begin their own personal relationship with God by trusting Jesus Christ as their Lord and Savior.

Many of the longer works in this book are written as spoken word pieces and may not necessarily be considered grammatically or punctually correct. However, you should read them as if I were standing on stage performing them live.

INDEX

A Tree..1

Stage Fright.......................................4

Something Simple That Makes Me Smile......7

Altar Whore (Deliverance)..........................9

Appreciate Christ................................. 14

No Sex... 18

To My Future Wife................................21

The Man Who is Devoted to Prayer.............25

When Life Happens................................ 28

What Am I Supposed to Say?...................... 30

Black is Beautiful!................................ 34

National Black Sitcoms Day?...................... 38

R.I.H. Dwayne Haskins Jr..........................43

Psalm 27:10.......................................46

Angels in Human Form.............................49

Learning How to Walk............................. 56

Help... 60

Growth.. 64

Love Anyway.......................................67

Live to Serve/The Vine............................. 69

   - "Live to Serve"................................. 69

   - "The Vine"..................................... 70

Die Empty.. 71

A Tree

When some see a tree,
they see an item blowing left
and right in the wind.
When I see a tree,
I see a tool used by God
to continually give life to man.
But isn't funny, clever, or even contradictory
how the same source of life for men,
Is it also the birthplace of death and sin?
I said isn't funny, clever, or even contradictory
how the same source of life for men,
Is it also the birthplace of death and sin?

See God made trees for his glory.
But man being corrupt,
chose to twist, roll it up, and smoke it
for their own enjoyment.
Now instead of seeing this object
as a symbol of good,
people see it as a reminder
of pain and torment.
Like the consequences of green envy
leaves that appear to be green
but turn out brown,
like chasing empty hopes and dreams
that at first make you smile
but then cause you to frown.

And if you think this is bad news,
hold on cause the worst is still coming.
See a tree reflects the dysfunctional church
of now, with its branches disconnected
by doctrines, money, plus egos,
and as these broken limbs get weak,
they become Satan's playground
for temptation and deceit.
Which eventually leads to our demise
and ultimately our defeat.
Well, that is until I took one last glance
at the trunk of the tree
and saw my savior hanging there
doing what needed to be done.

Ya see he bled, he cried, he suffered, he died.
All to revive the decimated roots
of this catastrophe,
all to restore a right relationship with humanity,
and to secure a place for us with him in eternity.
So the next time you're out enjoying the sun,
look up at a tree and give God praise
for all he has done!

Stage Fright

About to step up on stage
with a message for the masses.
Confident as I've practiced time after time.
Put the mic in my hand and then all of a sudden
the words escaped me.
(Like where'd they go?)
My voice tremblin', hands shakin',
knees buckin', thoughts racin',
wondering how I'm going to make it through.
Wondering if I messed up,
will the crowd laugh or boo?
So much pressure not to screw up,
and get this right.
But in case you couldn't sense it by now
I'm numb with stage fright.

Now some of you may feel like you can't relate
cause you've never been in the limelight.
But did you know a stage is not the only place
where you can experience fright?
Fear can occur when you're
around friends who mock God
and you choose to remain silent.
Like a snitch who knows
if they utter a word,
things are going to turn violent.

Or when someone influences you to do wrong
and instead of yelling out noooo!
You go ahead and try it.

Every area of life is a platform
and the choices you make in the scariest of times
determines whether you're requested to return
for an encore by those you adore,
or get thrown off by the ones you annoy.

Unfortunately,
no matter how much you rehearse,
or repeat each line,
this hindrance called anxiety may still lead to
your voice tremblin', hands shakin',
knees buckin', thoughts racin',
and a tinglin' in your spine.
To overcome this affliction,

do a praying sound check with Deuteronomy
31:6 and Philippians 4:6-9
knowing He's near and his peace
will step in right on time.
And start the performance with 2 Timothy 1:7
because God has not given us a spirit of fear
but of love, power, and a stable mind.

Something Simple That Makes Me Smile

Something simple that makes me smile?
The chirping of birds at dawn.
Don't understand their language,
but I love to hear their song.

The chirping of birds is a sweet-sounding hymn.
Proving everything is created to praise the Most
High.
The chirping of birds is a sweet-sounding hymn.
Awakening sleepy clouds in the morning sky.

The chirping of birds is such an interesting
thing.
Every 24 hours a new reason to rejoice.
The chirping of birds is such an interesting
thing.
Happily singing with such elation in their voice.

The chirping of birds, such a heavenly melody.
Their tone settles my spirit for quiet time.
The chirping of birds is such a heavenly melody.
Their tune eases my restless mind.

The harmony of birds as they soar in the air.
No need for work as plenty of food is all around.
The harmony of birds as they soar in the air.
No need to worry as God's peaceful provision
can always be found.

Something simple that makes me smile?
The chirping of birds at dawn.
Don't understand their language,
but I find hope in their song.

Altar Whore (Deliverance)

Sunday after Sunday,
I find myself in church
making powerful decrees about how it's over
between me and my struggles.
Only to find myself back down on my knees,
crying out to God saying please,
if you forgive me this time
I promise from these sins I'll flee.

Only to be back in the same position
the next week, month, year, or even day.
How foolish of me to take advantage of his
grace and his mercy in this way?
Knowing he'll come back for me one day
but I may not be ready.
Can't keep my feet steady, in one lane
I got to go back and forth
like two opponents in a tennis match.
One second I love God,
the next minute to the adversaries' schemes
I don't mind being attached.

Married to Christ, but cheating with the devil.
The resulting consequence makes me an altar
whore as I keep returning for more.

It's the same story, different Sunday.
Led to worship, pray and repent of emotion
Subconsciously unwilling to give
Jehovah Shammah all my devotion.
Instead, treating him like an absent father
never to be seen
so I guess it's back down on my knees
saying please, if you forgive me this time
I promise from these sins I'll flee.
Only to be back…
wait, hold up, got to fast forward,
tired of watching the same scene.
No change occurring, growing no closer to God
falling back into the same trifling behavior when
Monday comes.
Except now this habitual routine
has led to a psychological disease
as I think just running down to the altar
will help me start over.

You see my heart is divided, mind fickle,
life spinning out of control.
One of these ways I must let go!
So do divorce God and marry the devil?
Or do I recommit myself to his will
and take time to heal
from all those things within
that cause the Spirit within me to almost break?

Not a tough choice, the second option
I'll gladly take.
So I guess it's back down on my knees
and you know how this scenario ends
amounting to nothing
still tangled in a web of sin.
You see the issue isn't in how
but rather what I pray.
Instead of praying the same comfortable
forgive me chant
I need to get back down on my face,
go on an organized rant and tell God
how it's all my fault
and how I need to be set free.
Seems painful and unusual
but maybe this is the only way
from this adulterous chaos, I can depart.
Not realizing that deliverance,
I said not realizing that deliverance
should have been the first cry
to come from my feeble heart.

Deliverance is forgetting the pain
of what you've been through,
remembering the testimony that came about.
Turning away from those sins,
forgetting their name,
but being grateful God has
or is bringing you out.

It's changing your desire,
no longer wanting poison,
seeking the passion and the glory
he wants to possess.

It's breaking away from a vile heart
and with all you are telling him yes.
A gift like grace that often gets taken advantage
of but should be seen as another sign
of God's unfailing love.
Since we were the ones with our Barabbas
kind of lives who rejected him.
But he, being full of patience kept pursuing us,
when we were running after
someone or something else
replacing hymns of worship, songs of praise
for sounds of idolization and lust that were
determined to have us locked in our ways.

Deliverance, an emergency spare key that
unlocks God on a deeper level,
plucks us out of the hand of the devil,
puts back on our knees,
weeping before God,
wanting to be made new.
Causing us to sing songs that suggest God is
jealous for you and love lifted me.
An eleven letter word the angels

can't quite comprehend.
Since they don't see how God
can have affection for foul, corrupt humans.

Deliverance is another display of God's power
that he's in control and will never let us go.
A process God says we get to go through
because you'll never know, you'll never get,
you'll never fathom how much I love you.

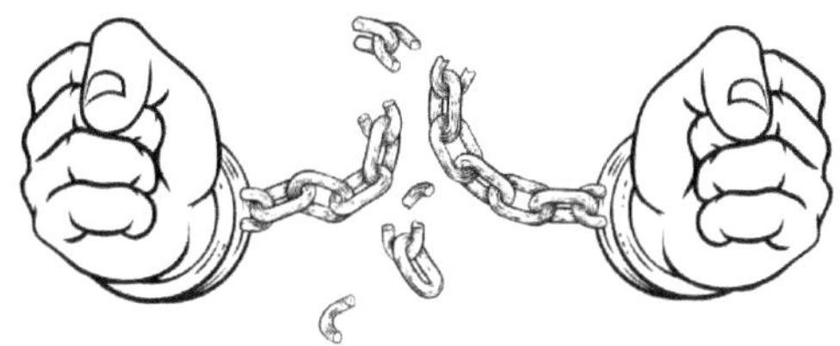

Appreciate Christ

He came into this world in the lowest of ways.
Sharing space with horses, donkeys,
and other fowl creatures.
All while being given gifts that symbolized
his death before his life even began.
As he grew into a man his challenges got worse
as he had to deal with doubtful followers,
ungrateful souls that after they were healed
had the nerve not to turn around
and tell God thank you!
A handful of religious know it alls
and a close friend who pushed for silver
just to watch him fall.
While most would complain
if they only had to face this kind of hurt,
Jesus had to endure being beaten on the cross,
getting mocked and treated like dirt.

But what's odd or better yet shameful,
is though he died more than 2000 years ago,
He still encounters disrespect today.
From other religions that devalue his worth
by suggesting he's just some prophet.

From those who claim to be his followers
but use and misrepresent his name
just to make a profit.
From media that portrays him as weak,
uses his name in vain and connects him with all
kinds of blasphemy and foolishness he would
never associate with.

From his own people, his own people
who call on his name only when they want
something and then live their lives
as if He doesn't exist.
Like he's their invisible genie,
only there to grant their every wish.
I find this repulsive and utterly disgusting
the way people act toward Christ.
But I'm serving notice to somebody
that you better appreciate him
cuz all that he did was not some pointless game,
attention getter, or a way to gain fame.

You see for every time he was scorned,
for every time he was rejected,
that made his desire to do the Father's will
that much greater.
For every lash, for each bruise,
for every drop of blood he shed on the cross
covers us from condemnation,

so we don't have to pay the full price for sins
like lying, cheating, stealing, and fornication.

Appreciate the one who chose not to stone
an adulterer and conversed with a Samaritan
in broad daylight while breaking bread
with prostitutes and breaking Sabbath Day
statues to work miracles and teach lessons
that prove women and the lame have the same
right to experience grace, mercy, and forgiveness
as "holy" men cause the Kingdom of God
doesn't exclude based on sexual sin, gender, age,
physical disposition, nationalism, racism,
or any other divisive ism that shapes the wicked
ideologies of this fallen land because the Gospel
is meant to restore and unify anyone who is
willing to abide by God's plan.

Appreciate the one who was God's plan
from the very beginning because he had
our victorious ending in mind
long before the snake would slither
his way into Eden, delivering temptation to Eve
making her believe she knew what was best.
While Christ chose to leave his royal place
of rest at the Father's right side
and take that transcendent step into time
forcing the clock to fall back

and move at his pace so the light of his patient
love could spring and shine in the face
of this dark and crooked generation.
While leading us to the straight way,
truth, and new life we obtain
when we receive salvation.

So will you choose to appreciate Christ
by giving him your soul
or die without experiencing the glorious
transformation you can behold
when you accept this revelation:
Jesus is Lord, Savior, King,
and Ruler of every nation
who can save anyone from hell
and eternal separation.

No Sex

No sex for me shawty,
cuz I ain't tryna take on none of the drama,
or end up with a disease.
The results of which my body
will be extremely displeased.

No sex for me shawty,
Wish I could present this
as the fresh fruit of purity
cause no one really wants to eat
the leftovers of celibacy.
But I can't take back the foolish choices I made
or purify the defiled beds
Mama always said to keep clean.

No sex for me shawty,
cause I've been restored
and I've been redeemed,
no longer allowing my body
to go through or be enticed by
any and every entrance of a girl's temple
No longer wasting my time, vision, emotion, or
adrenaline on taking cheap glances
at the adulteress fulfillment of some expensive
prostitute.
Since Christ never seduced

or wanted anything to do with a harlot
except for the part of their soul that cries out
I'm sick of my ways from them I surrender,
I'm ready to repent!

No sex for me shawty,
cuz I've seen it destroy the greatest of people,
destinies, and families alike.
How through this once pure
and yet now perverted stimulation
demons have leaped into the spirits
of the lost and even the believer
Causing them to desire the unnatural
and be under a constant cloud of regret
And the only time the sun shines
is when their bodies are intertwined
With their incompatible opposites
or their uncommon equals,
which leaves them positive and dying.
Even if their abomination doesn't come
with the letters of three
that spell out Sin Tragedy and Death,
or Health Invaded Viciously.
That's STD and HIV,
for those of you who weren't quite listening
since Ephesians 5:5 says no inside
or outside the church will make it to heaven
If from sexual immorality they do not flee.

No sex for me shawty,
until the day I marry,
if I'm even blessed with that chance.
A possible karmic consequence
for picking up the dice and taking a gamble
on what I thought was true romance.

No sex for me shawty,
this message I was scared to share
cuz I thought it might cause me to lose some
friends and supporters of my ministry.
But I'm just not gonna let the devil flee,
without declaring in a voice of victory
no sex for me.
Reunited with him and from this covenant,
I shall never again break!
And this little point I'm tryna get across,
just to let you know you can escape from this
oppressive form of a lifestyle you can escape!
Christ, Christ, Christ can set you free
and this I know because he did it for me!

To My Future Wife

Spent a good portion of my young time
searchin' for Mrs. Right
But every woman I come across
just catches an attitude
and put up a sign with big bold red letters,
w.r.o.n.g "WRONG."
Tired of being rejected but you won't hear about
it in a song.
I ain't even trippin'
since I know I've got to be selective.
Don't wanna get attached to a leach
that just takes bites out of my life
Instead, I wanna better half
who's worthy of being my wife.

One who can rock Ephesians 5:24
to the tee and model Proverbs 31
long after she's off the runway.
"A truly good wife is the most precious treasure
a man can find!
Her husband depends on her,
and she never lets him down.

She is good to him every day of her life
and with her own hands,
she gladly makes clothes
She is like a sailing ship,
that brings food from across the sea.
She gets up before daylight
to prepare food for her family
and for her servants.
She knows how to buy land
and how to plant a vineyard,
and she always works hard.
She knows when to buy or sell,
and she stays busy until late at night."[1]

This is the kind of woman I hope to make my
royal queen someday
but before I buy the wedding ring
there are some things you need to know.
Ya see I'm not perfect and I do have flaws
Grown impatient in some ways
because waiting for you was quite the task.
But prayerfully you can forgive my past
and help me start a true romance
that will forever last.
See I cherish the melanin in your skin,
and I don't care about your size, your past,
or where you've been.
The only thing that matters

---

[1] Proverbs 31:10-18, Common English Version.

is where you are in your relationship with God
and if you can help me get closer to his heart.

Our connection, just a display
of his divine reception
and how even when the noise of static
and problems causes things to seem dreary
we still can communicate clearly
cuz his attributes within us
can overcome the deepest pain
regardless of sunshine or rain
to the grasp of your sweet hand,
I will remain and I'll adore and lead
the same way Christ does for his bride.
So even if in our ways we slip and slide
and our hearts get separated in two
will find our way back to one another
because at the core of what we have
God's love will abide in spite
of whatever we go through.
These aren't corny words I'm expressing
but a revealing of my deepest desires
and longings for you a sanctified woman
whose life is a symbol of God's unfailing love.

You whose style and grace
is as beautiful as a dove,
got me pacing back and forth
as I think of you, my future unknown love.

You who will be the mother of my kids
the grandmother of my grandchildren.
You who I will grow gray with
let time run away with.
Speaking of which I'm way off in the future,
need to get back to the present with you
who I will always treat like an undeserved
present.

You who'll make me melt
every time you walk into the room.
Have me standing at the altar sweating
Cause I'm the nervous groom.
You who'll always have the key to my soul
pray you never make me change the lock.
You who my eyes will be for alone
and you who even though I've never seen or
viewed you in this life
have already stolen my heart.

I can't wait for the day you become my wife!

The Man Who is Devoted to Prayer

What man believes God is able to hear his every plea?
What man acknowledges who God is in every situation?
What man honestly confesses his faults?
What man thanks the Lord in all things?
The man who is devoted to prayer.

What man makes his supplications known?
What man learns to wait with expectation?
What man persists in intercession when there is no answer?
What man keeps seeking God when he seems to be absent?
The man who is devoted to prayer.

What man knows Jesus intercedes for him?
What man trusts the Spirit to pray when he's left speechless?
What man knows his purpose?
What man properly portrays his pain?
The man who is devoted to prayer.

What man is not afraid to shed a tear?

What man's dreams are not dashed by doubt?
What man knows the power of his words?
What man understands the impact of his actions?
The man who is devoted to prayer.[2]

What man maintains his composure in conflict?
What man humbly takes the high road?
What man forgives a cruel ex?
What man willingly abstains from premarital
sex?
The man who is devoted to prayer.

What man learns to love his wife?
What man lets his kids try things their way?
What man doesn't whine or complain?
What man sees the bright side in darkness and
rain?
The man who is devoted to prayer.

What man endures persecution with joy?
What man defends his faith without fear?
What man is filled with courage from the Holy
Ghost?
What man accepts the suffering he's called to
bear?
The man who is devoted to prayer.

---

[2] The first four stanzas are inspired by the A.C.T.S.
prayer method from *Too Busy Not to Pray by* Bill
Hybels.

What man lives a long and satisfying life?
What man fulfills his destiny?
What man will hear good & faithful servant well
done?
What man will see the face of the risen Son?
The man who is devoted to prayer.

How shall I become everything mentioned
before?
How shall I have a pure heart filled with love
forever?
I shall be a man who is devoted to prayer.

When Life Happens

Just wrote an awesome piece
for the first time in a while.
Something containing honesty
regarding my emotions and struggles
but it made me smile
as I reflected on the realities
of all that comes with this Christian life.
Christ, his sacrifice, my freedom
from the full price of sin.

But of course with the way life goes
it got deleted.
I could attempt to write it again
but maybe it was an act of divine intervention
to help me express my feelings at that moment
and then move on.
Maybe it was a lesson to stick to the intimate
process of a pen and pad
instead of the convenience of a cell phone.
I'm unsure of the purpose of this accident
but I know like everything else
it's working for my good.
I get to turn something that should have
frustrated me in to an experience
that will inspire me to get back into this craft.
Alas I must get some sleep as it's 1:13 am

and I can't wait to see where the day will take
me once I awake from this rest. Good night!

What Am I Supposed to Say?

What am I supposed to say,
when another black life
is needlessly taken away.
It's the same old mess on a brand new day.
This doesn't catch me by surprise
because there's nothing new under the sun.
Yet another black mother
mourning the death of her son.
No matter how many times this cycle is repeated
we refuse to be sensitized.
Eventually, America will pay attention
to the pain in our eyes,
the frustration in our voice,
and the anger in our steps
every time we stop the daily routine of our lives
to protest the loss of those left lifeless
at the hands of the law.

What am I supposed to say?
When the trauma and the pain
of being black in America
just won't fade away.
In a land where our ancestors
never asked to come
and the land where their offspring
don't always want to stay.

Tired of living with the fear
and anxiety of wondering
when their life may be taken away
at the hands of those meant to protect and serve.
It really irks my last nerve
but I've literally run out of words.
I mean what am I supposed to say
when it's just another day trying to survive
being Black in America?
What am I supposed to say
when another black life
is needlessly taken away?
It's the same old mess on a brand new day.
This doesn't catch me by surprise
since black lives don't seem to matter
in the eyes of those with the same pigmentation.
When we're all fighting for life on a planet
that says peaceful cohabitation
for our kind can only exist on a plantation.
So we beef over turf in neighborhoods we don't
own and will put a bullet in the dome
 of anyone we consider a threat
And could care less about the family
sitting at home mourning the loss of a loved one
because they killed our father, brother, uncle,
nephew, cousin, or son first.
Just another causality in a war
where this cycle of violence will last
as long as "stop snitchin'"

is the neighborhood slogan
and fear for one's well-being
makes silence the new golden rule.
Don't do unto others what might
send you to your grave.
Just modern-day slaves being self-exterminated
under the master's rule.

What am I supposed to say
when the life of another innocent child
is taken away?
Such a cruel joke for life to play on folks
with darker skin who refuse to take a day off
to ensure their offspring have brighter hopes
and dreams than they could ever imagine
than they could
Only to endure the nightmare
of seeing their kid lay lifeless on the ground
after being at the right place,
at the wrong time on a hot summer's eve.
When will the African Americans
do more than grieve when the suspect comes
from our community or looks just like us?
Where are the protests?
Where are the cries for gun reform?
Has this cycle gone on so long,
we no longer see this injustice as wrong?
Newsflash, a lack of action
other than violence is compliance.

Silence perpetuates the lie
that having black skin is a curse
but blessed are the peacemakers
who aren't afraid to raise hell on earth
in the name of justice because they want
to see God's face for all eternity.
But many stay quiet because they are too
ashamed to admit they have lost faith
and don't see how circumstances
can change in their present reality.
I mean what am I supposed to say,
when it's just another day,
trying to cope with being Black in America?

Black is Beautiful!

Black is justice.
Black is time.
Hate, love,
peace, war,
truth, lies,
divine.

Black is joy.
Black is pain.
Sunshine, heat.
Snow, cold,
rain.

Black is identity.
Black is a mystery.
Black is my history,
present, future,
my very being.

Black is viewing the world
through a different set of eyes
even though all mankind
has the same color pupils needed for seeing.

Black is culture.
Black Is talent.
Being black is a gift,
when others suggest our presence
on this earth doesn't matter.
Constantly striving to shatter our visions
and dreams with the blade of injustice.

Black is protest.
Black is civil unrest.
Black is wrongful arrest
guiding some beyond the jail cell
straight to the hands of death.

Black is grief.
Black is sorrow.
Black is hope for tomorrow!

A lifestyle rooted and grounded in Christ
when captors who once hung us
on branches with leaves
taught their ways to future species
who use their power
to legalize substances and ideologies
capitalizing on weaknesses that leave us hanging
high off tree and feening for whips and chains.
So this slave mentality we unfortunately
maintain, tarnishing the work of our ancestors
leaving their efforts to seem vain

even though physically freedom
it appears we have obtained.
But we have been set free in Jesus' name
So this truth I can proudly proclaim.
BLACK IS BEAUTIFUL!

Because it's the pitch black darkness
right before the son's rise.
Mixing the purity of his atonement
with the shedding of his blood.
The brown ugliness of the dirt of our sin
with the pink penetrating fury of his passion.
The amber of his anguish as he cried
"Eloi Eloi Lama Sabachthani
My God, my God, why hast thou forsaken me?"[3]

The green of his envy as the cross he chose not
flee
Rescuing the apple of his father's eye and the
core of his jealousy
the blue of his godly mourning
With the indescribable goldenness of his
heavenly ascension the place we all want to see
the some glad morning
because it's our predetermined
safe haven from this colorful spectrum
that is so dark and yet so bright
it leaves some blind to the fact

---

[3] Matthew 27:46 King James Version.

that when this mysterious potion
is swirled together used to create
an elegant portrait on a blank canvas
where all spectators see
is the glowing radiance of black.

And that's what makes black lives beautiful.
The fact that God can take all the chaos
and mess of our human existence
and use its obscure content
to create something marvelous.
Yes, that's what makes black beautiful!
So the next time you're feeling down
about who you are or all the flaws and travesties
you see within society, remember that in Christ
we are fearfully and wonderfully made
and BLACK IS BEAUTIFUL!

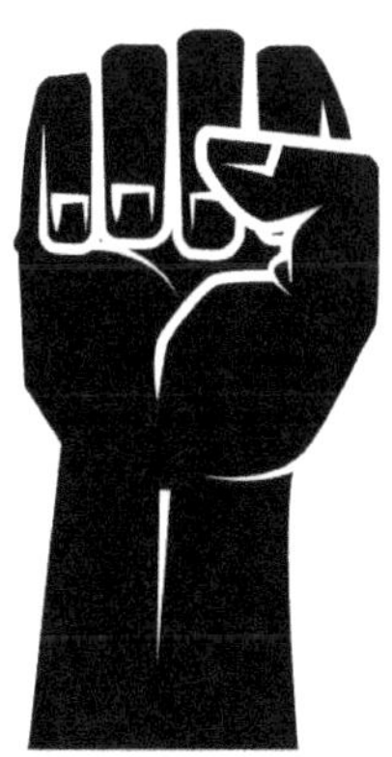

National Black Sitcoms Day?

Quick shout out to the Veterans on this holiday
who protect and serve this country every day.
Not to take away from their accolades,
but why do we have so many national days?
Why do we have to honor something every day?
It's obvious I'm kind of annoyed
but I'm really feelin' some type of way
when I realize that there is no such thing as a
National Black Sitcoms Day.

Like why not take the time to celebrate the ones
who make us laugh after a hard day,
give us commercial breaks to go grab a tissue
and wipe our tears away or release anger
and other emotions that help us express
frustrations that can break the human heart
but somehow mend them back together by the
end of the episode giving us a reason to smile
as they remind us that everything will be ok.

So today I ask you to consider giving these
actors and actresses their just due for the roles
they played on camera regardless of what they
have to endure when away from the limelight
because they used their gifts to inspire many

in the black culture to make a difference in this
broken world.

Shout out to a *Different World*
for showing me that college is possible,
respect *The Jeffersons* and *Cosby Show*
for their influence in highlighting
the black families' affluent side
or shows like *Good Times* and *Everybody Hates
Chris* that show us no matter how difficult the
struggle we can overcome financial adversity if
we stay together because *Family Matters*
no matter how much siblings may fuss and fight
like Sean and Marlon on the *Wayne's Bros*
or DeeDee and Roger on *What's Happening*
or how Roger use to annoy Tia and Tamera
on *Sister-Sister* but was always there as a friend
regardless of how many times they won't dare
to go out with him proving *Living Single*
is much better than being more than Friends
when friends of the opposite sex have pure
intentions and aren't afraid to show they care.

Whatever happened to shows like
The Fresh Prince of Bel-Air, The Parkers,
or *The Sinbad Show?*
That teach kids who grow up in a single family
or foster homes that they're never alone

even if their fathers aren't present in their life
because there will always be someone like
Uncle Phil, Uncle Bernie, or Uncle Curtis
in their House of Payne and an Aunt Viv
or Auntie Ella with hella patience to deal
with a knucklehead nephew from Philly
or more complex issues like a crack-addicted
niece or a son going through a divorce,
or a *One-On-One* glimpse into the life
of a single father raising a teenage daughter
while trying to excel in his career as a sports
anchor, I couldn't imagine being a man like
Keenan, a news broadcaster and the anchor
and *Roc* for *My Wife and Kids* after she dies,
keeping this *Proud Family* together through the
support of friends and loved ones providing it
takes *All of Us* to thrive as a community,
personally, professionally, and academically.

Shout out to Principal Greer and Vice-Principal
Steve from *The Steve Harvey Show* teaching the
world that black leaders can run schools with the
perfect balance of friendship, grace, love,
forgiveness and excellence even if society has
low standards for students who come from
low-class environments, and no class was more
fun for students in Oakland who were *Hangin'*
with Mr. Cooper when he was a substitute

teacher and didn't switch up on him when he
followed his childhood dream of playing
in the NBA but wasn't good enough to sit
on the bench as a substitute but being cut
from the league was the exact thing he needed
to dedicate his life to the needs of students
at his old high school who loved to cut class
and hang in there with them through tough
seasons to help them win a state championship.
There's no sweeter victory than *The Game*
that makes up for every downfall and major L
that prepares you for success.

Big ups to Tracie Ellis Ross in *Girlfriends*,
Blac-Ish, and *Mixed-Ish* for showing that black
women are the boss and that you should never
try to categorize, place in a box, or minimize one
part of their being because there are so many
facets that comprise their identity it will take
more than a lifetime to explore.

I can't believe I've learned all these lessons
from black sitcoms proving TV can do
 more good than harm.
So no I will not stay calm, I will not be silent
I will not be satisfied until black sitcoms
get there just do!

So thank you to *The Proud Family, Family
Matters, Family Reunion, The Bernie Mac Show,
Sanford and Son, The Parenthood, One on-One,
Half-In-Half, Sister-Sister, Living Single,
All of Us, The Jamie Foxx Show,
The D.L Hughley Show, Malcolm and Eddie,
Martin, Marlon, My Wife and Kids,
The UpShaws, Black-Ish, Black AF, Mixed-Ish,
Keenan, Cousin Skeeter, That's So Raven, Roc,
The Fresh Prince of Bel-Air, Corey in the House,
House of Payne, The Paynes, The Game, Amen*
and several others that my mind and tongue
can't seem to agree on their actual name
but who deserve their flowers just the same.
Thank you for taking the time
to inspire your fans in so many ways.
Hopefully, the world will come to acknowledge
your greatness and honor you with
a National Black Sitcoms day!

R.I.H. Dwayne Haskins Jr.

There's a saying that says
"the good die young."
And today, why is the question I'm left askin'
when I think of Dewayne Haskins Jr.
Like how could someone so young
in the prime of his life
24 years of age, May 3rd 2022
would have turned 25,
no longer be alive?
It's as if fate was a mischievous cornerback
that illegally intercepted the course
of his destiny.
I wish God would have stepped in like a referee
thrown a flag, called a 15 yard penalty
and ejected fate from his game of life
allowing him to play on so he could grow
into all he was destined to be.
The sports world should feel robbed
because he had potential far beyond
what our finite minds
could comprehend in this galaxy.
I don't consider it ironic
that we live on one of the arms of the Milky way
because it's with his arm
many rivals Haskins would slay
while a star Quarterback at Ohio State.

And even though his first stint in the NFL
came with some hell
he still had the determination to prevail
and kept digging his way to a second chance
until he found his opportunity with
the black and gold,
possibly being the 8th black starting QB
to be in the Superbowl.
A story I would have loved to see unfold
but that is not how God
wanted him to be known.
See his legacy extends far beyond
his athletic ability
he was a son, brother, husband,
a man devoted to community
and so much more than many critics
 could ever realize
because they only cared about how many times
he made supporting crowds roar
in between the lines of a football field.
Forgetting to exercise empathy and feel for a
human carrying the weight of the world on his
 shoulders all with a smile
I wonder if in his shoes
they would dare to walk a mile?
But glory, glory, hallelujah
 he can lay those burdens down and rest
as we reflect on how he ran his race,
accomplishing his purpose

with such class and grace.
A style peers and teammates hope to emulate
until they reunite with him one day beyond
heaven's gate above,
until then I know they'll forever cherish the
memories and thought of his name with love.

R.I.H. Dwayne Haskins Jr.[4]

---

[4]This poem was inspired by the *Brother From Another*
podcast segment "Gravity of Dwayne Haskins' Death"
described by Charles Robinson.
https://www.youtube.com/watch?v=YfhUcLfTTNY
Host Michael Holley and Michael Smith and contributor
Charles Robinson stress the importance of honoring the
humanity of and extending grace toward athletes when
discussing what they've done in their careers. Writers must
be mindful of an athlete's humanity. This is because
whether alive or deceased, athletes still have families,
supporters, and teammates who know them beyond their
athletic achievements, and they need to be depicted in a
respectful manner.

Psalm 27:10

I cannot imagine losing a parent.
But with each passing day
this possibility becomes more apparent
as my adopted mom is 85
and my biological mom is 52.[5]
I don't know what I'd do without either of you.

I cannot imagine them leaving this earth
though one did not give me life through birth
both have always been there for me.
One taught me how to be all God made
me to be, showed me how to put others first
and handle every situation with integrity.
The other taught me to be confident in who I am
not to depend on any woman or man,
and how to be a boss in this world
using my left hand.

Though I know heaven will be their new home
my heart will still feel empty
like a house after thieves commit a robbery.

---

[5] The terms biological mom and adopted mom are
used just to provide a clear explanation for how I
have two mothers. To me, they are both Ma.

Guess that's why my timeline saddens me.
Too many have lost a parent
over these past few years.
A child's deepest fear
because even if we beefin'
We know that love and compassion
of our parents are still sincere.

Who shall we turn to now
for counsel and wisdom?
Who shall we run to for a hug
or to hear stories about life "back in my day"?
Who else can be overheard
crying out to God on our behalf late at night?
When everyone else is doing wrong
who else will encourage us
to stand up for what's right?

While I'm glad I don't need answers
to these questions at this time
I know someone is grieving over their mom
and/or dad at this very moment
and though there really aren't any appropriate
words to utter amid grief and loss
take comfort in knowing that the Lord
will hold you close.

Yes, God will hold you close.
He will wipe away every drop of your tears,
calm all your deepest fears,
wrap his loving arms around you,
carry you when you don't have
the strength to walk,
speak through you when your heart
is too broken to talk.

Yes he is a father to the fatherless,
a mother to the motherless,
a guardian to the orphan,
a companion when you need a friend.
Yes, He'll be everything you need
in just the right way
and though their absence hurts
and may sting for quite a while
with God by your side just know
somehow you'll be okay.

"Even if mother and father abandon me, the
Lord will hold me close" (Psalms 27:10, NLT).

Angels in Human Form

In Memory of Donte & Charmika

Donte:

March 27 will always be a hard day for me
Nearly 17 years later
I've never really gotten over it
I'm learning to live through it.
Most people don't even know
about this part of my life
waking up around 5:30 am in the morning
to see my little brother laying dead
on our bedroom floor.
Oh Lord this is an open sore
that was never properly mended
but the older me is offended
by the fact that the younger me
tried to conceal these feelings.
But since it's your birthday
and I can't be with you in the present
I feel like it's only right to rewind the time back
17 years to March 27, 2006.
You were 12 years old, little did I know
this would be the last year
I'd get to see the joy within your smile
so bright it could light up in a room

the way you would when you'd hear my voice
showing me you cherished my words
and presence even though
you didn't have sight nor speech.
Still, your presence captured very essence of an
angel in human form.
Ain't nothing in my life been a norm
since you went to be with Jesus.
But you served your purpose
and ran your race well
though you were wheelchair bound
and depended on the help of others
to get around and function.
But when you were around
there was never really any tension
and I miss knowing how you felt
the peace of God
everytime Ma turned gospel music on
and you'd make a joyful noise
until your last days.
Because even in a state of pain
you understood the mention of Jesus' name
has the power to make every care fade away.
So on today, your birthday
I just want you to know
the memory of your face
is still fresh in my mind
though things will never be the same

and we've gone through some rough days since
you've been gone
Knowing you're smiling down on us
from heaven makes everything ok.
Donte' Moses Preston still loved, still missed
until I see you again in heaven.

Charmika:

November 16 will always be a hard day for me
9 years later I've never really gotten over it
I'm learning to live through it
Most people don't even know
about this part of my life.
Getting a phone call around 7:30 in the morning
To hear my big sister is no longer living.
Still haven't forgotten the shocking daze
of what I've heard.
Oh Lord, this is an open sore
that was never properly mended
but the older me is offended
by the fact that the younger me
tried to conceal these feelings.
But since it's your birthday
and I can't be with you in the present
I feel like it's only right to rewind the time back
9 years to November 16, 2013.
You were 29 years old, little did I know
this would be the last year

I'd get to see the joy within your smile
so bright it could light up a room
The way you would when you'd hear my voice
showing me you cherished my words
and presence even though
you really couldn't speak.
Still, your presence captured
the very essence of an angel in human form
and ain't nothing in my life been a norm
since you went to be with Jesus.
But you fulfilled your purpose
and ran your race well
though you were wheelchair-bound
and depended on the help of others
to get around and function.
But when you were around
there was never really any tension
and I miss knowing how you knew exactly
what time it was tough you couldn't express it.
You would have the whole house in a playful
uproar as you would make a playful noise until
*General Hospital, Oprah, Wheel of Fortune or
Jeopardy* was on the television.
I miss knowing how you felt the peace of God
every time the choir sang at church
or Mama turned gospel music on
and you would make a joyful noise
until your last days.
Because even in pain

you understood that the mention
of Jesus' name has the power
 to make every care fade away.

So on today, your birthday
I just want you to know the memory of your face
is still fresh in my mind
though things will never be the same
and we've gone through some rough days
since you've been gone.
But knowing you're smiling down on us
from heaven makes everything ok.
Charmika Carter Preston still loved, still missed
until I see you again in heaven.

I live in a world where people stop and stare
at those born with disabilities
because we don't look like
what they consider to be the norm.
But what if I told you people with disabilities
are simply angels in human form.
Sent to teach us lessons,
like how to be grateful
for the smallest blessings
in the midst of challenges and adversity.
Daisy thank you for showing me
how to enjoy life to the fullest.
I don't think there were but a few moments
where I didn't see you with a smile

or laughing at something funny.
But the funny thing about getting older
is you start to see things differently
that's how I want others to feel
about those with disabilities.
See we are not the result of some curse,
 the consequence of some mistake or accident.
We are a blessed, heaven-sent gift
presented to the world so that the power of God
can be seen through our struggles and triumphs,
good days and bad ones.

See we are angels in human form.
Sent to be a blessing that teaches others
how to exhibit compassion, patience, mercy,
empathy, long-suffering, how to be comforting,
courageous and show resilience when others
count us out and overlook our brilliance because
they lack the intellect to see how God uses
foolish things to confound the wise.

See we're born this way so God's light shining
within us can open the blind spiritual eyes of
those who don't trust that he's real
because they can see him in the natural.
So, if from our physical and mental deficiencies
God chooses never to heal
I just ask that he gives us the strength to live
each day to the best of our abilities

and represent him well as his angels
in human form.

55

Learning How to Walk

Most kids can't remember learning how to walk
because they've been doing it long before they
could talk and their memories were not strong
enough to hold the space necessary within their
minds to capture this moment.
But I remember it vividly because walking for
me is nothing short of a miracle.

My earliest memories are of me being confined
to a wheelchair at the age of three
having to depend on someone to push me around
or carry me everywhere I needed to go.
The doctors believed I may stay this way forever
but thanks to prayer and clever technological
advancements within medicine,
I have a different story to share.

So how does one go from being
wheelchair-bound to freely placing his feet
on the ground with each step?

Let me tell you, it was quite the process
with the performance of several medical
procedures, the awful instinct of anesthesia,
days in the hospital, nights of taking medicine
to soothe the aches and pains of being
in a full-body cast,
the thrill of returning for checkup appointments
knowing this won't last too much longer,
the need to get stronger requiring botox shots
physical therapy, motivation and support
from all of those who choose to care for me,
the need for me to get stronger requiring that I
learn how to stand and maintain my balance,
strength increasing with so much jubilation,
my progress feeling like graduation
as I forsake some wheels for a walker
and though I've never been a trash talker,
you can find me in a copy of the 1999
or 2000 Maryland Gazette
participating in a race or was it a walk-a-thon?
Either way, you should see the smile
on my face as I enjoy a taste
of freedom in my movement
that skeptics didn't think possible,
but I'm living proof anything is possible.
You can overcome any obstacle with prayer
and determination and even though this process
was never easy it felt like a celebration
as more therapy and Botox shots

loosen muscles and help me progress
to wearing AFOs and walking with crutches
though I never use my battle with cerebral palsy
as a crutch to keep me dependent on others
or make excuses that stop me
from being all I can be.
Though sometimes I did grow weary
with the mundane routine of therapy, surgery,
and botox shots,
I'm sure I would have knocked back a few shots
if I were legally old enough to drink
as at the age of 14 I grew strong enough to walk
with a cane and while that part of my life proved
nothing would ever be as simple and plain
as the days before my adolescence
15 years later I still consider it a blessing
and though there's hardly a day
where I don't feel some type of minor ache or
pain in my lower extremities
you can still catch me with dimples on my
cheeks and a smile on my face knowing I've
come so far in this race
but still have so much further to go as these
beautiful feet have the privilege of spreading the
Gospel of peace all over the place
as I limp along.
Jonathan McReynolds taught me through this
song that I can glorify God even with my limp,
my weakness because his joy is my strength.

Yes, the joy of the Lord is my strength.
So pay me no mind during Sunday service
if you see tears falling from my eyes
or if you see me up dancing and running around
the sanctuary like I'm crazy,
I promise you I still have my sanity,
I can't help but express my gratitude to God
when I reflect on my story,
and all the things he brought me through.
I'm a living testimony of healing in the process
and my suffering shall never be in vain
because it gives me more opportunities
to bring honor to his name.
If I never outgrow this cane
my suffering shall never be in vain
because I'm the once lame child he chose
 to use to remind the world not to take
the blessing of walking for granted.

Help

The most difficult reality for me to accept
when it comes to this life
is the fact that I need help.
It frustrates me knowing that I
can't rely solely on my own strength
and ability to make it through each day.
As a stranger stretches forth
their hand in assistance,
I hesitate and choose to keep my distance,
as this form of love I'm not willing to embrace.
It's not my fault I can't receive affection
I'm guarded for my own protection
as my ego cautiously warns me
not to entertain this act of charity.
Seeing as how I don't want to be perceived
as weak because of my disability.
See, help to me is just a
hassle exemplifying limitless pain.

What do I have to gain
from being known as one who walks
with a cane, limps with every step,
and seems to fall more often
than a leaf caught in the swift,
cool whisper of an autumn breeze?

Lord please, tell me what I have to gain
from being portrayed as meek
and needing help to accomplish
the simplest work.

Honestly, sometimes it makes me weep
as crippling thoughts play out in my mind
wondering if these deficiencies
will forever hinder me from meeting the man
I was predestined to be.
I plead, asking God to remove these infirmities
reminding Him of Psalm 103
where the psalmist declares
He'll cure all disease
of this I'm glad cause help to me
is just a plot limiting expected healing.

Why am I like this?
I mean, why do I take such offense
to the idea of assistance?
You'd think I'd appreciate it
since basketball is my favorite sport
and I consider myself a point guard at heart.
So I know how beautiful the art form
of an assistant can be
when an offense is flowing smoothly
Like the ShowTime Lakers running a 3 on 2
fastbreak back in the 80s,
it's simply Magic!

But it's oh so tragic,
how I let my pride keep me broken.
Now I understand why Jesus asked the lame
man if he wanted to be made whole.

Because some would rather find contentment
in complaining about their condition
rather than enduring the healing process,
they need circumstances to change
and are afraid to pick up their mat
and fulfill the responsibilities
that come with their supernatural transformation.

So today, I've decided to change my attitude
and embrace compassion when a stranger
stretches forth their hand in assistance
Because help is *humans encouraging lonely
people* out of isolation and into community
covering and comforting them in prayer
when the burdens of this life
they can no longer bear on their own.
No, I cannot do this alone.
I need Jesus and therapy,
both physically and mentally,
if I am to be spiritually healthy.
Cause even Jesus had help bearing his cross
during the hour he was most weary.
Yes, I need friends, family, and anyone else

who is willing to humbly endure loving people
where they are because we've all been hurt
or shall I say *humiliated, underappreciated,
rejected, traumatized,* and need to be healed
or shall I say: *hugged, encouraged,
acknowledged, loved, esteemed, defended.*
Thank God for help![6]

---

[6] Inspired by the book *Help* by Stephen Arterburn.

Growth

As a baby crawls,
takes a step and stalls,
takes a step and stalls,
to gain the strength and confidence
needed for walking without falling.
Likewise, a Christian crawls
takes a step and falls,
takes a step, and falls,
to build the faith and obedience needed to trust
God and live according to his calling.

Like a chick depends on its mother for food
and shelter during its first seasons,
then departs from the nest
to experience life on its own
for natural reasons.
Christians must get to know God for themselves,
and not rely on their parent's
relationship as a way to receive blessings
and out of ignorance waste inherited wealth.

As a patient places their health in the hands
of a hospital to make and keep them well,
a Christian must submit to the authority of the
church for spiritual guidance and maturing,
despite the fact that everyone has a flaw
and leadership has been known to fail.

Like a lion in the wild hunts, lurks,
and seeks to make a meal of other beasts,
a Christian must pray, provide help
and serve to seek the salvation
of the greatest and the least.

These four similes appear to be simple
elementary truths everyone should know
they're actually levels, processes, and steps
everyone has to climb in order to grow.

Growth isn't a five-minute jog,
or a quick little race.
It's a road with many a mile
that each life must conquer at its own pace.
It's a class that helps us
acquire a lot of discipline,
it's a humbling experience
like getting embarrassed
or having to go to God
and admit all your sins.

Growth is dessert and a valley
meant to dry up all you use to be
leaves you feeling soaked
like you're drowning in misery.
It's a method that God uses to strip us
of an ugly unintended reality
and reveal our true beauty.
It's an age where the world isn't dressed up with
invaluable accessories like some kind of toy.
Rather a complex piece of art,
where those who appreciate the smallest
details of life can find joy.

Growth is the bridge that helps us overcome
sinful habits and petty fights
that brings about tension and keeps veiled eyes
from seeing our light.
Growth is the ladder that enables us
to reach closer to God's heart.
Growth is the comforter that allows us
to let go of anxiety about death
and embrace our finish.
Knowing that once we're in our new glory
with the Father above
we'll be basking in his never-ending
unfailing love.

Love Anyway

I'm learning that even if
I don't particularly like someone,
or they don't particularly like me
for whatever reason,
I still have to speak, be polite, and kind.
Regardless of how I feel.
Because it's not about me
but the God I represent.
So for this former attitude
and vengeful mindset,
I must repent.

I can't say I love God
and not show love and respect to all people.
It's difficult, yes but I'm gonna practice it!
This is part of growth and maturity,
security in who I am as a man,
as a child of the Most High.
I don't have to take lowly steps
outside of my character,
stooping to someone else's level,
bringing joy to the devil.

No, I must rise!
Because it's God's name
I refuse to compromise.
At the cost of getting my point across
forfeiting the opportunity to lead every soul
to the cross that can set them free one day.

So whether I'm hated, have been wronged
or you've led me into dismay,
I've made the decision
that I'm gonna love you anyway.
Because when Christ I hated, wronged,
and chose from him to go astray,
He still loved and chooses to love me anyway.

So let's strive to love each other anyway![7]

---

[7] Inspired by Romans 12:9-21.

Live to Serve/The Vine

"Live to Serve"

Learning to be selfless by
Investing in others and
Voicing opinions when necessary to
Encourage all generations.

Taking the time to mentor and
Offer sound advice to the youth.

Surrendering to the need for humility
Expecting to be the example people need
Realizing I don't know it all and can learn more
Viewing life from unique vantage points while
Empowering the lonely and broken.

"The Vine"

Transforming lives for Jesus Christ by
Helping restore the community and
Encouraging youth to live out their purpose.

Vocalizing the Gospel
In every space and opportunity by
Never ceasing to pray, preach and serve with
Energy, empathy, love, and eternity in mind.

Die Empty

Dear Lord,

Thank you for taking the time to hear my plea.
I understand that one day the casket will be
the new home for my lifeless corpse
that will be its tenant until Christ returns
or time causes it to rot away.
But either way, all I can ask
is that before you let the coroner
place my 5'3 temple in this hollow vessel,
just grant me the grace to die empty.

I can imagine the casket responding
sarcastically, thinking how much more useless
can you be without breathe in your body?

But when I say die empty
I'm not talking about a lack of air in my lungs
but singing the written songs yet to be sung.

When I say die empty
I mean giving all I have to every task
without worrying about the reaction
of the crowd but giving my best
so my spirit can be proud
and my soul awards me
with a standing ovation
when I say die on empty.
I'm talking about considering my life worthless
letting Christ be my source of motivation
so I can spread the Gospel without trepidation.

Lord, grant me the grace to die empty.
I'm talking about not even one last drop
of a good drink left in the container
yet still hoping it will magically reappear
when I open the refrigerator
because I need something to quench
my thirst on a hot day-type empty.
Given all I have to give,
literally no energy left to live
because I left it all out there on the field
for four quarters and overtime
in order to obtain the sweet taste
of victory type empty.

Lord don't let me leave this earth
until everything you've placed within me
is conceived through some gift, or ability
that will help me serve my community
and help someone else give birth
to the vision you've placed before their eyes.

Lord, don't let the casket be my new residence
until I realize my full potential
and every talent you've called me to steward
is multiplied 2, to 5, to 10 to 100 times over
so I can bring you a good return
on your investment.
So I can hear well done good
and faithful servant
cause I don't want to die full of useless woulda,
shoulda, coulda's, or excuses
because they hinder me from doing your will.

So whether I die peacefully, tragically,
or for my faith be killed,
do not let my bones yield to the casket
until I've fulfilled every purpose
and assignment you have for me.
Until I've discipled others
so they can walk in their destiny.
Until there's no more work left for me.
One day I shall die but let me live
to declare your works faithfully
and may those left to celebrate me

joyfully agree that I left this life empty.